101
Questions
to Ask Before
You Get
Remarried

H.NORMAN WRIGHT

HARVEST HOUSE PUBLISHERS
EUGENE, OREGON

Many of the questions to ask before remarrying are similar to questions important for first-time engagements. Some of the questions, discussion points, and insights in this book have been drawn from H. Norman Wright, *101 Questions to Ask Before You Get Engaged* (Harvest House, 2004).

Cover by Dugan Design Group, Bloomington, Minnesota

Cover photo © Monkey Business / Fotolia

101 QUESTIONS TO ASK BEFORE YOU GET REMARRIED
Copyright © 2012 by H. Norman Wright
Published by Harvest House Publishers
Eugene, Oregon 97402
www.harvesthousepublishers.com

ISBN 978-0-7369-4906-4 (pbk.)
ISBN 978-0-7369-4907-1 (eBook)

Printed in the United States of America

21 22 23 24 /VP-CD/ 10 9 8 7

Contents

Establishing a Solid Foundation

Today blended families have moved into the majority. Unfortunately, the divorce rate of second marriages is higher than first marriages. Lack of preparation and the abundance of unexpected problems contribute to this problem. *101 Questions to Ask Before You Get Remarried* is for you if you're contemplating marrying again, whether you are divorced or widowed. It's designed to address significant issues in advance so you can discuss differences in views and styles and establish a solid foundation of harmony before you make that lifetime commitment. This will give you a leg up for finding solutions when differing opinions and conflicts arise. You'll also discover how to better work together to resolve issues and face the world as a couple.

What will you find in this helpful book? A balance between significant and penetrating questions for you to discuss and brief, informative selections of beneficial information. The questions asked in this resource come from my experiences as a Christian counselor to thousands of couples, from conducting many marriage seminars, and from being a widower who is happily married again. Dozens of individuals who have experienced remarriage also contributed questions based on their experiences. Contemplating these questions and talking through your answers will hopefully help you create a relationship that will stand the test of time.

Here are some realistic expectations to consider if you're in a serious romantic relationship and thinking about getting married.

- You can expect your second marriage to be successful if you dig in and work for the long haul.

- The new marriage will be tougher than a first marriage. It will be complicated, exasperating, and tiring at times.

- You can expect a slow building process.

- You can expect some "old scripts" at times, but you are also writing a new script every day.

- You can expect to want to run from it every now and then—but you won't.

- You will be able to solve the problems that often cause a "run or rust" mentality in second marriages.

- You can expect this marriage to be different because you've learned many things from your previous marriage and how it ended.

You will be asked many questions in this book. You may feel some are repetitive. They are, and there's a purpose for that. The second time you see a question, your answer may be different because of the context or wording. This will help you dig a little deeper into your thoughts and expectations. Also, some of your ideas and thoughts will change as you work through this book and consider your views and your partner's views.

Can Romance Survive Practical Questions?

So often we get caught up in our emotions and how wonderful it feels to have someone next to us when we attend events, travel, watch television, and go to church. Time together can be so exciting that we overlook how much we don't know about the person. And sometimes we don't even realize how much we don't know.

Even though time is valuable, spending it now to really get to know your potential life mate will do one of two things. It might save you from a lot of heartache and misery if you discover there are some values you can't work out or idiosyncrasies you don't want to live with. Or discussing these questions now will solidify your relationship, improve your communication, and help ease you over difficult spots when they arise because you've already covered them.

During my many years of being a Christian counselor, I've heard so many people say, "The person I married was not the same one I dated or honeymooned with. It's as though he (or she) changed overnight. What happened?" The answer is simple. The person asking the question married a stranger. There was either courtship deception, naïveté, not enough questions asked, marrying for the wrong reason, or marrying too soon. Here's a good illustration.

Let's assume you have sufficient money to purchase a new car. You go to the auto mall where there are 16 dealerships. The lots are filled with cars of all makes, models, colors, vintages, and prices. You pull into the lot, park, and stroll over to a great looking car. It's a previously owned model (which means *used*). It's been around the block a few times. But you really like the way it looks and smells. You get in, and it's very comfortable. There are a number of fun gadgets, including a GPS.

A salesperson comes up and asks if he can help you. You respond, "You sure can! I want to buy this car."

"Great. What would you like to know about it?"

"Know? What's there to know? I saw it. I've checked it out. I like it. I want it. Let's draw up the paperwork."

"I can do that. Do you have any questions about its warranty, performance, estimated mileage, or the GPS? And since it's a recent addition to our inventory, we haven't even put a price on it. Don't you want to know how much it's going to cost?"

"Not really. All I know is that I want it. And you don't even have to wrap it!"

Would you buy a car in this way? It's doubtful. In fact, it's almost ridiculous because you'd be going into it blind. So no, of course you'd ask questions. It's too big of an investment to not be careful. You don't want to make a costly mistake.

Unfortunately, many people who get engaged do a similar thing. They don't ask enough questions. They like what they see, how they feel, what they enjoy doing, and that's all that counts for the moment. Their hearts flutter, and that's enough, right? After all, asking questions isn't very romantic…and they may not like the answers.

The fact is that at some point in time you will discover the answers to the important relationship and lifestyle questions, whether you ask them or not. Asking them *before* you say "I do" will help you evaluate your relationship and either save you from heartache or confirm you're heading in the best direction. Having more information gives you a better base for making wise decisions.[1]

Yes, asking questions can be awkward and even a bit scary. And if the answers aren't satisfying or raise red flags, it's painful to slow down or end a dating relationship. But it's even more painful to break off an engagement and cancel wedding plans or get into a marriage full of conflicts. Hopefully, the questions and information in this book will help you say, "Yes, I really know this person. I feel comfortable in moving ahead" or "I'm glad I asked these questions. Now I won't pursue this relationship. It's time to move on."

Any Red Flags?

How long and how well do you know this person you're considering as a marriage partner? Most of the questions and thoughts in this book have been derived from people who discovered the answers *after* they were married. They were shocked, dismayed, and some even felt deceived. Many of the questions are direct and blunt so you may feel hesitant to ask them. You may think, "I can't ask that!" You may worry you might offend your potential life partner. Or you may think, "Asking these questions seems so unromantic." Or perhaps you don't want to hear the answers (ignorance does not create bliss).

Remember, you're thinking about marrying this person you're involved with. Few areas should be off-limits. You may feel awkward asking about debt, past romantic relationships, or the difficulties the person has had with his or her children. You may even be worried about answering these types of questions yourself. The truth is that you can ask the questions and discuss the answers now or not ask them and discover the answers later. It's your choice. I believe it's better for you to be in charge of when you find out because, as I said earlier, you will eventually.

Along with the questions offered in this book, you'll find suggestions and helpful guidelines for open discussions and things to watch for gleaned from my counseling practice and people willing to share their stories. Some may sound like warnings or cautions. They are. Now is the time to look for red flags or concerns so you can discuss them, work through them, or, perhaps, decide to slow down or end the relationship. Although it can be very painful to apply the brakes on a relationship, it's even more agonizing to not do it and end up in a rocky marriage.

I've shared the following story from a friend at my conferences, and people have found it helpful. I believe you'll find it useful too.

In searching for the perfect mate, it has taken a long time for me to discover that there really is no such creature out there. Everything is found in degrees of compromise. *Can I live with this or can I accept that?* When I have found one that fits most of my criteria and parameters, then the question is, *Will I fit hers?* It's extremely difficult trying to find someone where all the gears seem to mesh into place without a lot of grinding.

I think one of the things I find valuable in dating now is all the experience I have compiled over the years from different situations. I have reached the point now, in my 40s, where I feel I finally know some of the answers to the questions I didn't even know to ask in my 20s or 30s. But to this day, I am still adding and updating my list of questions.

If there are any bits of advice I could give anyone who is looking for their ideal mate, it would be these. Ask questions of anyone you date. Store their answers in your memory bank to see if the answers continue to be consistent with their actions. If something appears to be a red flag, confront it. Don't let it slide as "not that big of a deal." Interact with the other person's friends (in group settings), such as on camping trips or skiing trips or by playing interaction group-type games. If possible, spend time with the other person's parents or children (and if any red flags come up, don't ignore them because their children are products of their environment). If there are ways of seeing how the other person will handle pressure situations...put them in it (this way you are able to see how flexible they are or can be and how they hold up under pressure).

Build a real friendship but stay out of bed. Pray together, have similar values and interests in things, come to know the other person's faults and if you can accept them, watch to see how they treat their pets, and continue to interview them right up to the last moments before marriage...

And as hard as it may seem, if that inner voice tells you

that you are making a mistake, at least stop and listen to it. Be willing to pull the plug or at least put things on hold until issues can be clarified in the relationship—right up to the day of the wedding. It is my feeling that I would much rather be very embarrassed and cause hurt to both of us by putting things on hold—or walking away from the relationship right up to the final days before the wedding—than suck it up, be mad, and live in misery for the rest of my life. Why marry when maybe you know deep down inside that things are not right or that small things are adding up to be big things, but you don't know how to confront them? Why marry just because you're afraid you might hurt the other person by confronting them? A lot of this stuff will come to the surface through premarital counseling. Know ahead of time that some people are able to mask or hide things. If you don't ask specific questions, they may feel, "If you didn't ask, I didn't lie." Never assume anything.

A good thing to remember is that you can't reshape, remake, or reconstruct another person. You can't get gold out of a mine filled with lead. I've seen people who don't get along at times but assume it will get better once they're married. They usually end up frustrated and critical, feeling betrayed and trapped. Some people feel called to be reformers. They like to reshape others—or at least try to. In doing so, they ease their own pain by not looking at issues in their lives.[2]

Every Morning at Breakfast

In the book *There Goes the Bride—Making Up Your Mind, Calling It Off and Moving On*, the following suggestions were made. Please consider them carefully:

- "If you have mixed feelings about engagement, don't! You need to be certain. If you get engaged, listen to the feelings, especially numbness or dread or just plain wrongness. These shouldn't be there."

- "Engagement is a serious state. Listen to these words: 'Dating is one thing, but signing up for the rest of your life is liable to give anyone a few second thoughts. The challenge is deciding if you're suffering from garden-variety cold feet or what I call "Frozen footsies"—a much rarer malady.'"

- "Don't feel pressured into engagement or marriage because your biological clock is ticking faster and faster. As one woman said about making a mistake of becoming engaged, 'I was turning thirty and that expiration date stamped on my forehead was flashing so brightly that it blinded me from all the signs.'"

- "If you're thinking of committing your life to someone for the rest of your life, identify the nonnegotiables. Don't do this after the fact. Consider these nonnegotiables:

  ▸ If your partner hurts you physically, don't proceed. It won't get better.

  ▸ Emotional abuse is more difficult to identify, but it involves lack of respect, controlling, etc.

  ▸ Does the other person put you before their parents' wishes or are they controlled by their parents? The scriptural teaching of 'leave their mother and father' includes emotional as well as physical.

  ▸ Don't plan on marriage fixing your current problems. It compounds them. Work on fixing them now, but if you can't repair them...

  ▸ If you feel inhibited in what you talk about and can't bring up your needs and concerns now, it won't improve. Try new approaches now.

  ▸ If you find yourself saying 'I love him or her, but...' why would you think of proceeding?"

- "Remember, a wedding is exciting but it lasts for just one day. Is this the person you want across the breakfast table from you every morning?"[3]

Here's another insightful story about romance that reveals some important considerations when it comes to dating and considering engagement or marriage.

> My wife had died from lung cancer. While cleaning out her closet of clothes, I realized that the beautiful dresses I had bought for her that she loved wearing were now meaningless to me...that it was the person *in* the dress that made the dress come alive and not the dress on the person making them pretty. It was at that point that I prayed to God, "Make my life have purpose for You, give me direction in where You want me to be so it will have real meaning."
>
> In the last stages of her cancer, my wife told me that if she wasn't going to make it, she wanted me to not spend the rest of my life single. In going through a period of time of grieving, I came to a point of feeling alone. But where do you even start at 55 and having had an incredible marriage? I had truly found my soul mate when I found Sherry. She was a godly woman, pretty, smart, loving, loved the outdoors where we fished and hunted together. She was sweet, kind...She was everything I had dreamed of in a wife and more.
>
> It had been through many years of prayer and patience that I had finally found the love of my life, and now she was gone...I had a huge void in my life. It had taken years to find a lady like Sherry, but when I found her I can remember thinking to myself after six months of marriage, "Now I know a little of how Adam felt when God introduced him to Eve...This is so good, and this is what marriage is supposed to be like!" Sure, we had our little everyday problems like every marriage has, but I really can't picture marriage any better than what we had nor a wife as special as she was.
>
> So in beginning to date, the first three or four dates didn't have a chance, and neither did the next three or four—and really, it probably wouldn't have mattered what the women's qualities were or how godly they were. I was trying to find another Sherry, and no one could ever fill her shoes. The one thing that I wanted more than anything if I were to find someone that I could fall in love with again was to have

purpose for God. Almost four years had gone by, along with an untold amount of first and last dates, when I met Kathy. I had met her on a Christian internet site when she wrote me...We wrote each other and then talked. She seemed like a possible good match, so we carried it to the next step...to meet in person. I asked her where she would like to meet, and she gave me the location. It sounded like a familiar place, but it wasn't until I got there that I realized this was the exact place that Sherry had brought me on our first date. Now what are the chances of something like this happening? It was Sherry's favorite place, it was also the same beach where we spent our last anniversary together. Now this was almost too eerie. I was wondering at the time if this was some kind of a sign from God, and if it was the passing of the baton—and I was the baton.

Sometimes I have found that we try to look so deep in trying to find a sign from God that this is where He wants us to be, but in dating I found it to be more coincidence than a message from God. This was one of those times where I was looking more for the divine than listening to reason.

Kathy and I dated for more than a year and a half. We became very involved in both church and weekend missions into Mexico. It was something I had so much wanted to be involved in because we were giving so much to the children of migrant workers. When we first found this camp, it was like one of those commercials you see on TV asking for donations for sick children. Their noses were all running, and they had flies all over their faces. They were malnourished... It was just an extremely sad sight to behold. It was exciting for me because for the first time in my life I really felt this was a real purpose to get involved in, and it was with someone I was having feelings for. Kathy had lost her husband about the same time Sherry died, and she felt that missions were her calling. It was feeling more and more like a match that truly was made in heaven.

I was so happy in what I was doing with her that I failed to notice some of the red flags that were popping up—like the relationship was all one way, and it was either her way or it was going to be the highway. I really felt that this was where God wanted me to be, so I continued to compromise...It was nothing like what I'd had with Sherry, where we were both givers and couldn't out give each other...Now I had found a taker, and, being a giver, I just gave and pretty much didn't get anything in return other than how I was being blessed in seeing so many children and adults coming to Christ from what we were doing.

I share this only because I really thought this was where God wanted me to be, and I accepted things in the relationship that I shouldn't have. We married, but the old adage that you always hear, "If they are not nice to you while you are dating, why would you think they will be nice to you when you are married?" came true.

Another thing I learned from all of this was just because a person claims to be a Christian doesn't mean that they will always act like one. Another is even though they act one way at church in front of friends, that doesn't always mean that that's the way they really are behind closed doors. Also, just because you might date for a year and a half, if they don't let you into their life other than what is on the surface, you really don't know that person. In other words, you want to feel like you know that person warts and all. If they're not willing to show themselves as less than being perfect on the surface, know that this is a major red flag. Don't go through it without addressing that issue with that person.

It is easy to look in the rearview mirror and see the things that you couldn't see when looking forward. The biggest bit of advice that I can give someone when dating after you lose a spouse, be it through death or divorce, is not to take anything for granted. Don't let little things go without addressing them because they grow on you and become major. When they finally come to a head—and they will—they're harder to resolve or you will just be in denial and confrontation becomes harder.

It has been a little over four years now since I went

through that divorce. In my dating, I'm taking advantage of my past errors. I will only date someone who is a giving person, someone who shows that she has the fruit of the Holy Spirit, and that she is a Proverbs 31 lady to some extent.

One last piece of advice is to date through all four seasons, and spend a lot of time interacting with both your friends and hers. Listen to what your friends have to say. Stay in prayer that God will keep your eyes wide open.

Warning Lights

There are more warning signs about relationships. Take a look at the following points. They may be indications that marriage is not the best direction for you to take right now.

- Are you asking, "Are you really sure you love me?" again and again? It's an indication of low self-esteem. Counseling would be better than marriage.

- If most of your time is characterized by quarrels and disagreements that never get resolved, marriage will make them worse.

- If you plan to live together before marriage, don't. It hurts your chances of a lasting marriage.

- If your partner is like a parent you don't get along with, why would you want to marry that person?

- If your partner is all for your interests and activities, but then reacts to you spending time on them, this won't get better in marriage.

- Don't marry just for sex. Physical intimacy alone won't keep a marriage together. You need the emotional, social, spiritual, intellectual, and recreational intimacy as well.

- How do you feel if you spend a day with your partner just hanging out and talking? If it's intolerable, why are you together?

- If you haven't recovered from a previous relationship, you're not ready for a new one.

- If your partner has an addiction and isn't in a recovery program, you're not their therapist. And promises to reform aren't a basis for marriage.

- If the two of you are totally opposite, what delights you now will probably be a pain in the neck later.[4]

I hope the information and responses have given you guidance about whether or not you should pursue the relationship you're in. That's the purpose! All of them are meant to be spoken out loud to your potential mate. His or her responses can either be verbal or written. I recommend you set aside an ample amount of time regularly to allow for discussion as you go through this book. After the questions, I offer some insights and, at times, suggestions on how to deal with some of the answers.

Hopefully, you'll enjoy learning more about your partner and you. Maybe after you've finished this book, you'll be even more convinced that engagement is right for you. Wonderful! Or perhaps you'll question whether this relationship is "the one." Either way, keep reading and asking questions. It's better to discover the truth now.

Previous Relationships

Remarriage—what will it hold for you? It's a major step not to be entered into lightly. Making your next marriage work will take more effort and investigation than your previous one. Marriage is a major decision for every person at any stage of life. As you plan for this new marriage, it's very important to realize and consider what effects your previous relationship will have on this new one.

Our past experiences affect us more than we realize and often more than we want them to. It is possible, however, to live free from the hurts, wounds, and disappointments of our pasts, but we can't do that by ignoring them. Looking back at our former marriages may elicit feelings and thoughts we hoped were gone forever, yet this step is necessary to properly plan and prepare for life with our future partners.

There are reasons we make poor choices in selecting new marriage partners. One of the issues that can interfere with both the selection and the growth of a new marriage is unresolved issues or losses from the past. These need to be faced and solutions found before they have an opportunity to take root and flourish in your new relationship. Losses and hurts interfere with our wisdom and decision-making in selecting new partners.

Let's consider the factors that contribute to making poor choices. As you read, ask, "Do I connect with any of these?"

- Ignoring negative information or insights you have about the person. Denial has no place in a relationship.

- The right questions were not asked. (Can you think of any questions you've wanted to ask but have been hesitant to do so? If so, ask them now!)

- You haven't spent the time you needed to get to know the person thoroughly.

- You wondered about some behavior or beliefs of your partner, but you dismissed them as not important. You talked yourself out of your concern. Never rationalize away your concerns or you'll pay later.

- You allowed the pressure of others to influence your choice. Are these individuals really experts?

- You weren't sure what you really wanted in a partner so you opted for what was available.

- You made your decision based on feelings rather than facts. Your right brain didn't consult the left side of your brain.[1]

A loving and fulfilling remarriage will depend on how well you prepared yourself, your future spouse, and your children from prior relationships.

Is the prior marriage over? Do you think that's a strange question? It's not really. Many marriages end in court or death, but emotionally they linger on for years. If the previous marriage is alive in any way, it will be a hindrance to the new relationship.

- How frequently do you have contact with your former spouse, if any, and in what way? What is the purpose of the contact? What feelings do you experience on these occasions?

Some believe they can "just be friends" with a former partner. But why do they want to be? Is the relationship really over? Why spend time with someone when there is no future? And if your new partner is really interested in you, it would seem his or her time and energy would be directed toward you. If your partner says there are no feelings regarding the old relationship, ask again. It's rare to be neutral.

- How many times have you been married (including annulments)?

- How long ago was the divorce(s)?

Sometimes a partner may *forget* to tell you about a brief marriage or annulment. If so, what else aren't they telling you? Sometimes people say, "Well, the first one really didn't count because we were so young, and it only lasted six months." A marriage is a marriage. If they were formally married, did they attend a divorce recovery group or counseling after the breakup? It is necessary. How long ago was the divorce? It usually takes two to three years to recover.

Les and Leslie Parrott describe the interaction between new relationships and previous ones this way:

> The biggest challenge will be that you will soon discover you've married two people: your new spouse and their former partner. The former partner may be deceased or live a thousand miles away, but they will be there. They will be there, for example, on former anniversaries. They will be there when your partner recalls something they used to do or say. Trust us, a former spouse, no matter how distant, still roams the halls of your new home. So go into this marriage with your eyes open. Talk about it. Let your partner know it's okay to talk about. Get this fact out in the open, and as you

explore it, learn what makes you uncomfortable and what doesn't.

You may encounter the ghost of your partner's former spouse in a variety of places—in the kitchen, on vacations, and so on—but allow us to mention an area that is very personal: your love life. It is not uncommon for someone in your situation to have curiosities about your spouse's former lovemaking. This can be a difficult issue that festers for years if not exposed. Don't keep your concerns about the topic bottled up inside.[2]

In remarriage there is also another cast of characters in addition to husband and wife. You are also marrying your spouse's family and friends. People bring routines into a remarriage that were developed with a previous spouse. Often they subconsciously expect the new spouse to know and accept those routines.

People also bring memories into a remarriage, both positive and negative. When everything is going well with your new partner, your memories from the previous relationship are negative. You recall the shortcomings. But when things are not going well with your new partner, you may tend to idealize the former relationship. Remarriages are fertile grounds for comparison.

- How would you describe your former spouse and your present partner?

- List 10 adjectives that describe your former spouse:

  1)   6)

  2)   7)

  3)   8)

  4)   9)

  5)   10)

- List 10 adjectives that describe your current partner:

  1)   6)

  2)   7)

  3)   8)

  4)   9)

  5)   10)

- Using the lists from the previous question, indicate with a check mark the adjectives that also describe you.

- Underline the following descriptions that apply to you. Place a check mark by the ones that apply to your former spouse. Circle the ones that apply to your current partner.

Abusive physically	Cries a lot
Abusive verbally	Depression
Aggressive behavior	Difficult at work
Alcohol use	Drug use
Compulsive behavior	Impulsive behavior

Insomnia	Self-esteem low
Lazy	Sleeps too much
Loss of control	Smokes or chews
Overeats	Suicidal behaviors
Overworks	Suicidal threats
Perfectionistic tendencies	Type A behavior
Pornography	Withdraws from others
Procrastinator	Worry
Risk taker	

If divorced, you may have contact with your previous spouse because of children. Conduct this relationship as a joint-parenting venture or even as a business arrangement. Children *will* affect your new marriage. And the effect will be extensive if there are unresolved issues or bitterness between you and your previous spouse and other family members.

Hopefully, denial is not part of your life. Denial keeps remarried spouses and their new marriages from becoming all they can be. "Denial" means "to avoid or reject reality." It is necessary to grieve for the former partner as well as for the former marriage. Whether it ended in death or divorce, there was loss. Grieving helps the pain of loss fade away. Denial dulls the pain of anger, but the anger itself doesn't go away. It's buried alive but remains full of negative energy. You may think you have worked through your feelings of hurt, bitterness, anger, jealousy, and fear, but they may return from time to time. They must be faced and experienced for what they are. Denying these feelings prevents healing.

Don't be surprised if some of these feelings emerge occasionally during the first few years of your new marriage. Events, dates, special occasions, and places can bring back a flood of memories. You may wonder, "What's wrong with me?" Nothing! A new relationship, with its growth and adjustments, can also bring back the past. You may have to face and resolve your feelings in new ways. Talk through your emotions with your new partner. Share this adjustment process together without being threatened by past relationships.

As you learn to share your past, your present, and your future together, the pains and hurts of the past will be easier to handle because you're not doing it alone.

If you experience difficulties with your former spouse, such as a power struggle, animosity, or an uncooperative attitude, you may need to work out a policy or plan with your new spouse to help you handle these difficulties. This plan should help you:

- prevent your previous relationship from having a negative effect upon your new marriage

- keep any ongoing differences or complications from hurting the children from the first marriage and any future children from the new marriage

- at least on your part, create respect and positive behavior between you and your former partner

If you are in need of such a plan, describe what you can do to help accomplish your goals. Let's consider some of the feelings you may be experiencing at the present time. After completing the following section, don't hesitate to seek help in developing a viable plan.

- Fear can paralyze any person. You may fear that the past will repeat itself. Indicate on the following scale the amount of fear you have. After that, describe in detail the reasons for this fear.

0	5	10
Not at all	Moderate	High degree

- Another feeling is guilt—the feeling that says "I did something wrong." Guilt can occur because of unfulfilled expectations from the past, from disrupting your children's lives, or from breaking commitments. Do you experience guilt over your previous marriage? Even if it ended because of death, guilt can be a factor. Identify the amount of guilt you feel on the following scale. Then describe the reasons for the guilt.

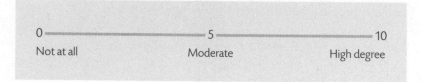

0 ————————————— 5 ————————————— 10

Not at all   Moderate   High degree

- Another frequent emotional companion is anger. You could be angry about the past or the present. If anger is not properly and harmlessly released, who knows when it will spill out and contaminate your new relationship? Sometimes anger takes the forms of resentment and bitterness. Let's identify the residue of anger that may be present in your life today. Indicate on the scale the amount of anger in your life over your former relationship. Then clarify the reasons for the anger and what you are doing about relinquishing that anger.

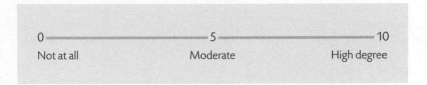

0 ————————————— 5 ————————————— 10

Not at all   Moderate   High degree

- What has been the response and attitude of significant other people in your life to your divorce? Please name them, describe their negative and positive responses and how their responses affected you.

Person	
Positive Response	
Negative Response	
Your Response	
Person	
Positive Response	
Negative Response	
Your Response	

- Describe the steps you've taken toward forgiving your former spouse and yourself. What have you done to turn your former married relationship into a healthy unmarried relationship? Remember, unresolved clutter from your previous marriage will affect the amount of clutter in your new relationship.

Rebuilding

It's important to identify the steps you've taken to rebuild your life after your previous marriage ended. Let's consider what you've learned and how you've grown.

- How long has it been since your previous marriage ended?

- Who were the support people you developed to help you through this time?

- How do you feel about yourself now compared to how you felt at the end of your previous marriage?

- What have you learned since the end of your first marriage (skills, vocational changes, etc.)?

- What have you learned from your past marriage that will help you in your new marriage? Please be as specific as possible. You might include what you've learned about yourself—your needs, your feelings, your goals, your flexibility, the way you handle stress, the way you handle another person's anger, how other people are different than you.

- In what ways will you be a better partner because of what you've learned? (Please list at last six.)

  -

  -

  -

  -

  -

  -

Relinking

"Relinking" is the stage of looking and planning ahead in a positive manner.

- If you have children, describe your discussions with them concerning your new marriage.

- Describe your children's feelings and attitudes toward your new partner.

- Identify your parenting style and methods of discipline.

- What are your future partner's parenting style and methods of discipline?

- What books have each of you read about remarriage and stepparenting?

- What decisions have you and your future spouse made concerning existing children and having children together in the future?

- How will your remarriage be affected by financial obligations from the previous marriage?

Money management in a remarriage can become a nightmare. If there are children from a previous marriage, financial support can become a burden to the new marriage. Consider this fact: Only approximately 1 in 10 children live with their biological father and a stepmother. Because of this, the typical remarrying father will enter his new marriage with up to 20 years of financial obligation. Each month he will send a check to his previous wife. If his new wife has her own children, he will also be helping to support her children.

Marrying Again

- What do you think will be your greatest challenge in your new marriage?

- Describe how your new partner is similar to and different from your former partner.

Similarities	Differences

Similarities	Differences

• Describe your expectations if you decide to marry.

What was the situation in your former marriage? Let's compare it to the situation with your prospective partner.

- How long did you know your previous spouse before you began to date?

- How long did you know your current partner before you began to date?

- What attracted you to your former spouse?

- What attracted you to your current partner?

- How long did you date your former spouse before deciding to marry?

- How long did you date your prospective spouse before thinking seriously about getting engaged?

- What were your reasons for marrying your former spouse?

- What are your reasons for considering marrying your current partner?

- What dreams did you have for your prior marriage?

- What dreams do you have for your prospective marriage?

- Describe the pattern of marital satisfaction in your previous marriage, filling in the appropriate months or years on the time line.

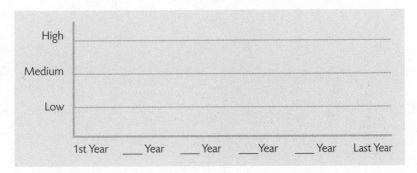

- Indicate on the chart and below when the major conflicts started, what they were about, and how they manifested themselves.

- What did you do to improve the relationship?

- Indicate on the chart when the decision to divorce was made, and who decided to go that route.

- How long did the divorce process take?

- Describe in detail how your divorce impacted and changed you.

- What positives will you bring into your new marriage from the previous marriage?

- What do you *not* want to bring into your new marriage? How will you avoid this?

- Chart the pattern of marital satisfaction you predict you will have in your prospective marriage.

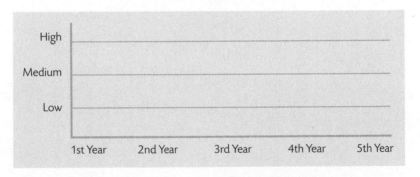

- Describe specifically what you will do to make this a reality.

- Describe the fears and concerns you have about your new partner and your new relationship.

- If you have children from your previous marriage, what will be the biggest challenges that they will bring into your new marriage?

Challenges with Children

Here is a sampling of what the future holds with your children in the remarriage. Have you considered these issues?

- What will you call former partners when they call or visit?

- What rules will you have for phone contact and personal visits by former partners?

- Should former partners be allowed inside your home? Should you visit in their homes? If yes, what rules will apply?

- How will you handle disagreements over the care of the children and activities in which they are involved?

- What will you do if one of the children or stepchildren wants to change residence?

- How do you feel about gifts or the types of gifts former partners may give to the children?

- How do you feel about gifts or the types of gifts former partners may give to your new partner (either to him or her directly or on behalf of the children)?

- What visiting privileges will you give to the relatives of your former partner who still relate to your children or stepchildren as part of their families?

- How will you talk to your children or stepchildren about your former partner's motives and actions that you believe to be unhealthy or wrong?

- What will you tell your children to say to a former partner when they are asked about your new family relationships?

- What will you say about your new family when you are asked by others about the new relationship?

- What is your plan for handling holidays, birthdays, and special occasions—including your desires and your former partner's desires when it comes to special events?

- What will you share with your children about the new relatives they will soon have?

- What additional issues might you need to work through or discuss regarding your children or your new partner's children?

- Describe how you have listened to and responded to your children's concerns about your future marriage.

3

101 Questions to Help You Develop Your Relationship

1. How long has the person you're interested in been single?

How long have you been single?

On a scale from 0 to 10, how comfortable are you being single?

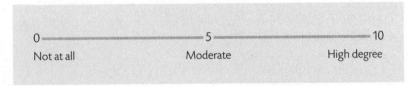

0	5	10
Not at all	Moderate	High degree

On a scale from 0 to 10, how comfortable do you believe your new partner is being single?

0	5	10
Not at all	Moderate	High degree

What are your thoughts when it comes to you and being single?

Many have not adjusted to being single again, so you might end up marrying someone who still has one foot in the previous marriage. It's also vital to accept being single and adjust to it without this being a driving factor to remarry.

2. What makes it easy for you to be open and vulnerable?

What makes it difficult?

Does your partner find it easy or difficult to be open and vulnerable? How do you know—what signs have you noticed?

The answers to these questions are a road map. You want to respond in a way that makes the person feel at ease in your presence. Give your partner every opportunity to be vulnerable or become vulnerable. Perhaps this is the first safe relationship he or she has experienced. Or perhaps the previous relationship makes it difficult. If vulnerability and openness don't develop and occur now, they probably won't later.

3. Approximately what percentage of your time getting to know each other has been through...

- texting:

- emailing:

- Facebook or other social media:

- telephone:

- face-to-face:

In today's world of technology, the doors of communication are opened wide. It would seem that now more than ever finding a quality person is possible. We can ask questions and get answers all day, any day, through many means. These means can be wonderful tools, but in the very important process of really getting to know people, they can also be used to mislead us.

Using technology, we often lose body-language cues, eye contact, facial expressions, and tone of voice—not to mention the big area of having the ability to *watch* how people live in day-to-day life. We only learn what they want us to know, which may not reflect reality. We need to build in opportunities to *see* who people are, ask the important questions face-to-face, and watch them interact with others.

Not only does this help us discover the real person, it also helps us gauge how this person will respond in future situations that are similar. The inner person is who we really are. We must cut through the initial social presentations, Facebook fun, email mystique, texting technique, and all else that may cloud our vision to get to know the inner person in potential mates.

4. How involved are you and your partner on Facebook or other social media?

What guidelines, if any, have you created for social media involvement after your engagement and after your marriage?

Facebook and other social media are extremely popular means of communication and social gathering today. Most of what they offer is positive. Like most everything else, there can be downsides as well. Couples need to set guardrails on their time and relationship on social media.

It's easy to reconnect with someone from the past and romanticize. It's also easy to flirt online. Committed relationships are vulnerable to all kinds of online and real-life threats because couples fail to set up proper boundaries of protection and accountability.

Be discerning about what you put on Facebook and other social media, whether it's information or photos. Be reserved and professional. Technology does affect relationships and can even change them. When Scripture says it's not good for man to be alone, it's not talking about connecting via Facebook or Twitter or other social media. It's referring to face-to-face contact and relating. Some couples communicate more by texting than by talking! Can you go without texting, Facebook, Twitter, or other social media in your relationship for a few weeks or even a month? Try it!

You may want to read *Facebook and Your Marriage* by K. Jason Krafsky and Kelli Krafsky.

5. What is your greatest fear or concern about being remarried?

What have you done to address this concern?

Have the two of you discussed this yet? If not, when will you bring it up?

Fears are normal, but they can bear scrutiny. Are yours realistic? Where did they originate? Are there good causes for them or just imagined ones?

Has your partner ever consulted someone to help put fears to rest or gain insights about them? If not, encouraging positive action is a great step.

It's better for both of you to identify your fears and face them now than have them brought up after the wedding. "Oh, by the way…"

6. What are five reasons a person would want to spend the rest of his or
her life with you?

-

-

-

-

-

What are three reasons he or she wouldn't?

-

-

-

These soul-searching and personal questions help you know how well
your partner knows him- or herself. What reasons do you have for being
together or not being together? The responses may elicit extended discussions. Can you predict your partner's answers? If so, you know your partner quite well.

One last thought: If your partner doesn't have answers to the second
question, be cautious. There are always reasons to remarry and reasons
not to remarry. Ask your partner and yourself these important questions:

- Why am I ready to remarry, and why are you ready?

- To what degree am I not ready, and to what degree are you not ready?

- I am right for you because…

- You are right for me because…

- Is there any way in which we are not right for one another? What do other people say?

Some reasons *not* to remarry are:

▸ If you feel like you *need* to remarry, don't do it.

▸ If you have serious, unsolved problems in your life, work on them. Don't try to solve them through getting a spouse.

▸ If you have doubts about someone you want to remarry, stop, allow more time, or back out.

▸ If you're not happy with your life, don't get remarried until you are.

▸ If you're not ready to take care of someone else, then take care of yourself first.[1]

▸ Love at first sight, having to talk yourself into believing you love the person, or thinking the love will come after you marry is a great reason to give yourself a lot more time to get to know the other person before marrying.

▸ "Rebound" is a reaction to something that occurred *before* rather than what is perceived as new love for someone else. If you still feel strongly about or feel hurt from a previous relationship, don't get into a new one.

▸ Make sure you aren't rebelling. Yes, even adults make decisions based on rebellion.

▸ Perhaps the most damaging reason is escape—wanting to be rescued from loneliness or debt or being single. If that's the case, don't marry.[2]

You want to marry from a state of healthiness rather than unhealthiness. Dr. Neil Warren said, "A marriage can only be as healthy as the least healthy person in that partnership."[3]

7. What have you learned from your previous relationships that will make you a better partner for someone now? What lessons learned from your previous marriage will help you in your next marriage?

What lessons has your partner learned through previous relationships that will help in your relationship?

Every previous marriage can be a learning experience. For some people, it makes them wiser. For others, it makes them wary. Note whether the responses tend to blame the other person. Did your partner learn more about the other person or about him- or herself in the previous relationship? What will he or she do differently in your relationship?

8. If you could have done something differently in your previous marriage, what would it have been?

What will you do differently in this relationship, especially if you marry?

Have you already implemented those changes in this relationship? Why or why not?

9. Describe your spiritual journey over the past 10 years, including high and low points.

Perhaps neither of you has ever thought about this or mapped it out. It's time to do so. What caused the low points? What contributed to the high points? Is there a pattern to the journey? Where would you each like to be in the next 10 years? What do each of you need to do to make it happen?

10. We hear a lot today about compatibility. What does this concept
    mean to you?

"Compatibility" means being capable of living together harmoniously
or getting along well together. It means to be in agreement, to combine
well. It also means blending together so a relationship enhances each partner's capabilities. A couple needs to work on compatibility in *all* areas of
their relationship. Those who desire to be compatible develop characteristics and skills that will help them achieve unity. They flex, stretch, adapt,
and change. There's no other way to build a solid, lifelong relationship.

P.S. Partial compatibility doesn't work very well. It leads to
     holes in the relationship. Becoming compatible is a devel-
     opmental process. If someone doesn't know what com-
     patibility is or refuses to flex, stretch, adapt, and change,
     how can unity grow?

11. To what extent do you see the ways you both communicate as similar?

In what ways are they different?

- What does the phrase "learn to speak your partner's language" mean to you?

Everyone comes to a relationship with his or her own language style, dictionary, and patterns of speaking. Some are expanders, and some are condensers. Some are ramblers (changing the subject often, not finishing thoughts, going around the barn several times), and some are bottom-line, right-to-the-point communicators. No styles are wrong; they're just different. People enjoy and relate best with those who are flexible enough to learn to speak their partner's language. Is this a new concept for you? Think about how it can apply to you and your partner. You may want to read my book *Communication: Key to Your Marriage* (2000) to learn more about this.

12. Is it easy or difficult for you to pray with a person you're in a relationship with? Explain.

Prayer is the foundation for strong intimacy in relationships. Praying together builds the other dimensions of intimacy. Author and psychiatrist Dr. Paul Tournier states,

> It is only when a husband and wife pray together before God that they find the secret of true harmony, that the difference in their temperaments, their ideas, and their tastes enriches their home instead of endangering it. There will be no further question of one imposing his will on the other, or of the other giving in for the sake of peace. Instead, they will together seek God's will, which alone will ensure that each will be fully able to develop his personality.[4]

Lines open to God are invariably open to one another. A person cannot be genuinely open to God and closed to his or her mate. Praying together especially reduces the sense of competitiveness in marriage. At the same time, it enhances the sense of completeness.[5] If you haven't prayed together yet, perhaps now is a good time to begin.

13. To what degree are you a saver or a spender when it comes to money?

• To what degree do you believe your partner is a saver or a spender?

Money is a major issue! How will you work out financial differences? There will be some, even if your general philosophy about finances is similar. If your partner is a saver and you are a spender, or the other way around, how will you respond to each other? How will you handle expensive purchase decisions? Work out in advance how you both approach and handle money—expenses, debts, church and ministry giving, savings, investing, disposable income—or you could be heading toward disaster. Les and Leslie Parrott, in *Saving Your Second Marriage Before It Starts,* point out:

> Money is the number-one source of conflict in marriage. And when it comes to second marriages, the potential for the fur to fly over financial issues is even stronger. Why? Because there may be houses to sell, alimony issues, inheritances, debt on one side or the other, and so on. The point is that money matters in second marriages are complicated. Very complicated. You will be deciding important issues like whether to have separate bank accounts, how your money gets spent, whether you work with a budget, how to save for retirement, whether children get an allowance and how much, which house will you live in, and so on. Of course, all this will be influenced by your previous marriages and how money was—or wasn't—handled.[6]

14. Will you help pay your partner's previous debts?

What will you do if your partner wants to go into debt to purchase an item…and you don't want to?

The greater the financial resources brought to a marriage, the more often couples sign legal premarital agreements. An agreement is also a good safeguard when one partner brings large debts into a marriage. If the spouse with the debt died soon after the marriage, the other partner could face financial disaster when the bills come. An informal agreement regarding debts can help couples better understand each other's attitude about finances, establish a coherent plan, and set up a framework for making decisions.

15. Who handled the finances in your previous relationship?

Who do you think should be the primary handler of finances in your current relationship? Who will be responsible for making sure the bills are paid on time? What will you base those decisions on?

Regardless of whether the two of you have great wealth or little financial resources, the question of who will handle current incomes and expenditures needs to be decided. Both of you have had a period of independent financial decision-making. Surrendering that independence may not come easily. And if one partner sees the role of money manager as a means of controlling the marriage or partner, trouble is sure to come.

When both of you were the guardians of the treasury in your previous relationships, how can you avoid a power struggle in your current relationship?

An agreement on finances reached during the engagement and prior to the wedding can lessen or eliminate tension as your relationship enters into its new phase.

16. How do you think income and expenses should be handled in your relationship? Will you keep your money separate or pool everything?

How will spending disposable income for gifts, vacations, home, and hobbies be decided, including choosing the appropriate amounts for items?

What will you do if your partner overspends or exceeds the budget?

How do you think your partner will react if you overspend or exceed the budget?

To handle monthly income and outgo, the best way is to work together to establish an agreement on the details. This needs to be established and settled *before* the wedding ceremony. Both of you must be satisfied that the plan is the best choice for your partnership and circumstances. One key to financial success is to discuss *everything* in advance.

17. How has your relationship with Jesus Christ changed since you've been in your current romantic relationship?

Did you think this was an odd question? There are several possibilities when it comes to answers. Perhaps there has been no change. It has remained the same. Is that because of the relationship or because you've stuck to your typical pattern? Or perhaps your relationship with Jesus has diminished. Is that because of the relationship? Is your partner struggling spiritually? Hopefully, both of you are growing spiritually and encouraging one another.

18. Describe what your life was like before you met your current partner.

Describe what *you* were like before you met your current partner.

Changes will occur in each of you in a relationship. Some are healthy, and some are not. Healthy changes involve making adjustments and accommodations for the other person. Unhealthy ones change the person you are. For example, if your personality was outgoing and socially active but you've become withdrawn, you need to explore why. If your family and friends say, "You're not the person you were before you became involved with that person," you need to find out what they're observing in you. Don't assume you know the particulars. Ask them for specific feedback.

19. Dreams and aspirations are very important. Have your partner complete this phrase, and then discuss them.

- "If I were to marry I would…"

- "If I were to marry I would…"

- "If I were to marry I would…"

- "If I were to marry I would…"

- "If I were to marry I would…"

Now it's your turn to answer this phrase.

• "If I were to marry I would…"

• "If I were to marry I would…"

• "If I were to marry I would…"

• "If I were to marry I would…"

• "If I were to marry I would…"

Your partner's response to this phrase is a window into his or her dreams for the present and the future. It may reveal information you've never heard before. You may be shocked, delighted, surprised, or reassured by what you hear. Being married is meant to enhance and enrich your life, not limit or restrain it in any way.

20. Ask your partner, "What questions about me have you wanted to
ask but never have?"

This could become very personal, and that's good. You may be surprised by your partner's questions. Above all, don't be defensive or offended.
Thank your partner for being open and vulnerable by asking. You may
want to answer immediately or reflect on the questions for a while.

Another thought—why didn't your partner ask these questions before?
Is it because your partner tends to be hesitant or reserved or because he
or she was concerned they wouldn't be received well? That's something to
think about and discuss.

21. What do you think are God's purposes for marriage?

Here are some thoughts on marriage from Scripture:

- "God created mankind in his own image, in the image of God he created them; male and female he created them" (Genesis 1:27). Marriage is to mirror God.

- "God blessed them and said to them, 'Be fruitful and increase in number; fill the earth and subdue it. Rule over the fish in the sea and the birds in the sky and over every living creature that moves on the ground'" (Genesis 1:28). Marriage is to multiply a godly legacy.

- "The LORD God said, 'It is not good for the man to be alone. I will make a helper suitable for him'" (Genesis 2:18). Marriage partners are to mutually complete one another.

God chose to reveal a part of who He is and His character through our relationships. Marriage gives us a picture of what God is like. And marriage is definitely a sacred union.

22. What are your beliefs about prenuptial agreements?

Do you have a will or living trust? What changes will you make to these when you marry?

Prenuptials often reflect a lack of trust as well as incomplete commitment. When you marry, you need to go into marriage with your eyes wide open but with the intent that you *will* be together " 'til death do you part." Establishing a living trust is a better option.

23. When do you experience loneliness? What messages do you tell yourself when you're lonely?

Loneliness occurs whether you're married or not. Are there times when you are with your partner and yet you still feel lonely? Too many people end up as "married singles" in their relationships, and this is the worst pain.

24. In a relationship, what part of giving of yourself do you struggle the most with?

Yes, it's a strange question, but one that needs to be explored. For some people, it's difficult to give of their time or money. Others find it difficult to share personal possessions, friends, or the limelight. Some people are gifted at giving themselves, while it's a challenge and chore for others. Many relationships are out of balance, with one person doing most or all of the giving. This isn't healthy. There needs to be balance.

25. What are your beliefs about pornography?

To what degree has pornography ever impacted or been a part of your life? Explain.

How recently have you viewed pornography?

A pattern of involvement in pornography is a problem. Most people today have run across soft- or hard-core pornography out of curiosity or inadvertently because of inaccurate film ratings or computer searches. The choice to pursue pornography will destroy a marriage. If your partner has struggled with pornography, recommend he or she seek help now. Don't accept a promise to "take care of it later."

26. If I were a doctor and you were describing your medical history, what would it entail? Include such things as accidents, allergies, hospitalizations, and diseases (including sexually transmitted ones).

Some individuals have been shocked to learn about serious medical issues *after* they married. That's when a person feels deceived. Some conditions may limit having children or determine where you can or can't live. Everyone's imperfect physically. It's better to learn about your partner's limitations and accept them fully now. And the same goes for your partner learning about yours.

27. If there is a significant age difference between the two of you, how might this impact your relationship in terms of work, exercise, sexual intimacy, retirement, and the possibility of being widowed?

This question may be uncomfortable, but it's necessary. It's better to consider these factors now than be surprised or confronted by them later.

28. If something *really* bothers me about my partner, how will I express it?

If something about me *really* bothered my partner, how would he or she express it?

The *way* we express our concerns to one another is important. Delivery can be everything. If you feel attacked, you'll probably be defensive. Some people tend to bottle up their feelings and concerns, but then they accumulate and often there is a blowup. The book of Proverbs gives us some guidelines:

- "A man who refuses to admit his mistakes can never be successful. But if he confesses and forsakes them, he gets another chance" (Proverbs 28:13 TLB).
- "Timely advice is as lovely as gold apples in a silver basket" (Proverbs 25:11 TLB).
- "Those who guard their mouths and their tongues keep themselves from calamity" (Proverbs 21:23).

29. What would the people interacting with you in your prior marriage
say about you?

What did *you* learn from them?

If others were consistent in what they said to you about your previous
partner, was it positive or negative? If you hear all positives or all negatives,
ask about areas they didn't share with you. Do you see the same traits, ten-
dencies, or qualities in your partner? Hopefully the prior relationship was
a learning experience for the best rather than one that warped the person's
view about the opposite sex.

30. What is there about my life and personality that concerns you at this
     time?

If you hear, "Oh, nothing concerns me. You're perfect," then love really
is being blind. Be extremely wary. No one is perfect. If you hear, "Well,
now that you ask..." and your partner goes on and on, that raises red flags
too. Why is the person still in a relationship with you? Why are you still
in a relationship with that person? A few concerns are a reasonable part of
the adjustment process. It's called "a growth experience." Talk it through.

P.S. If you're constantly hearing complaints and concerns
about who you are from your partner, you're involved
with "a reformer." He or she may also be a perfectionist.
Either way, the engagement won't be pleasant, and neither
will the marriage if it gets that far.

31. How has your relationship with God changed in the past five years?

How has your partner's relationship with God changed in the past five years?

Has there been spiritual growth? Is the spiritual part of your partner's life on hold? Has it diminished? What has he or she read? Has he or she attended any conferences? What is your partner's involvement in church? What questions does he or she have about God? What is his or her prayer life like? These questions are very important to determine where both of you are spiritually and to see if both of you are headed in the same direction.

Have the two of you read a Christian book together? If not, it's a wonderful journey to start now. Some of my favorite authors for reading as a couple are Ken Gire, Max Lucado, and John Ortburg. You may also want to read my devotionals *Starting Out Together* and *Before You Say "I Do" Devotional.*

32. How will you keep romance alive in your marriage?

What might interfere with intimacy?

What appears to be romantic to one person might not be to another. Your partner may have several ideas or ways he or she likes to show love, but they may not light your fire. It's important to discover what types of romance each of you enjoy so you can establish a good road map for keeping the flame alive. And, by the way, romance won't just continue or occur. It takes commitment to make it happen. And it helps to look your partner in the eye and say "I love you" every day. If this isn't happening now, don't assume it will happen after you marry.

33. Have you ever freely talked to your partner about sex? About what stimulates you and what turns you off? Do you feel embarrassed or too awkward to ask? Has your partner ever candidly asked you?

Many couples assume that people don't have to talk about sex since it "comes naturally." This isn't so. We're all different from one another, and we need to express our likes and dislikes rather than expecting or hoping that our partners will be able to read our minds or know intuitively how to please us. Your past marriage can also interfere because of comparisons or worries about inadequacy.

Marriage counselors often warn couples about sexual problems that may exist in a remarriage. Here are some of them:

- A know-it-all attitude based on previous experience.

- False assumptions about the opposite sex based on the former mate.

- Reluctance to communicate explicitly for fear of rejection (not verbalizing preferences).

- Old flashbacks appearing during intimacy, creating response problems.

- Difficulty in feeling "one" with the new mate. Sometimes emotional healing and unresolved guilt need professional help.

- Privacy problems if there are children.

34. What are five habits you're glad you have?

-
-
-
-
-

What are five habits you wish you didn't have?

-
-
-
-
-

Everyone has some habits or patterns. Are yours similar or different? How do you feel about your partner's habits? Can you live with them? Accept them? Has your partner asked you to help get rid of the habits he or she doesn't like? Any annoyance you feel about his or her habits now will intensify after marriage.

35. Describe the people in your life who are the easiest to get along with.

Now describe the people in your life who are the most difficult to get along with.

Which list is longer? Is your partner someone who has good people skills? If he or she struggles with others, are the two of you getting along well? If so, what is the difference? Is your partner a person who accepts responsibility for difficulties? Or does he or she project blame onto others? Does your partner have characteristics similar to the people he or she has difficulties with?

36. Ten years from now, where would you like to be emotionally?

How about spiritually?

How about economically?

What family size would you like to have?

Has your partner thought about his or her personal growth? If your potential life mate is content with the way he or she is, be cautious. It's easier to answer the last two questions, but the first two are more important for your future. If you're given general answers, ask for specifics.

37. When you are sick, how do you want others to respond to you?

When a significant person in your life is sick, how do you respond?

Illness is not something people usually think about before marriage. People have patterns of responses to sicknesses they've developed over the years, as well as a mixture of expectations and needs when they're sick. Many conflicts have occurred because couples have not discussed this before marriage. One or both of you may need to adjust your way of responding to meet the other person's needs.

38. What brings you the greatest satisfaction in life?

What do you think it is about you that brings the greatest satisfaction to the Lord?

This is a two-pronged question. For some, the answers are obvious, while for others it's a mystery. Do you have a difficult time with what brings your partner satisfaction? Can you see outward evidences of what he or she thinks brings satisfaction to the Lord? Is it a consistent growing pattern or an occasional event? If your partner responds to these questions with "I don't know" or "I can't think of anything," what does that say to you?

39. What are the "must have" and "must not have" qualities in a person you would consider spending the rest of your life with?

Listen carefully when your partner shares his or her lists. Do the items on those lists match who you are and what you have to offer? It's essential to clarify and verify these qualities in advance because they won't change easily and may eventually become demands. Sometimes "shopping lists" are reasonable, but sometimes they are not.

40. What is in your life now that you *never* want to change or that you would never be able to let go of?

This question gives you insight into your partner's values. It's good to know about these now. They might be major items or they might be insignificant. Can you accept them? Will they be a problem for you? Can you live with them the rest of your life? Where did these values or items originate? What makes them important? Are your values similar or on the opposite end of the scale? Similar values are one of the essentials for a quality marriage.

41. If you could ask Jesus to change an area of your life, which area would it be? How would you like it changed? How long has this area been a concern to you?

Were you aware of the area your partner mentioned? Has he or she ever considered asking Jesus for help in this area? This could open up a healthy discussion about the importance of your partner's spiritual life as well as give both of you guidance in praying for each other.

42. What has God taught you in the following situations in your life?

- Failure:

- Pain:

- Waiting:

- Not having enough money:

- Facing disappointment:

- Facing criticism:

Plan enough time for this discussion. It's not uncommon for a person not to have sufficient life experience yet for some of these to apply, but in time he or she will. Others have lives filled with these experiences. If you handle them differently, that's all right. These questions will hopefully generate additional insights for your partner and you.

43. How would you generally rate your friendships with those of the same sex?

- Easy—it's a snap.
- Whatever—I can take them or leave them.
- They're hard work but worthwhile.
- Discouraging—they let you down.
- Not sure if I've ever had a deep friendship.

Explain your choice.

We weren't created to live in isolation. Whether we're male or female, we need friends. It's important to like and respect your partner's friends. If not, conflict and taking sides may result. If you are "the only true friend they have," you could end up emotionally smothered by your partner. Neither of you can meet all of the other person's needs. After marriage, time with friends will have to be adjusted, but don't eliminate it.

44. To what extent does your former spouse occupy your thoughts—who he is, what she's doing, what he didn't do, what she might do, and so on?

45. Describe the emotional attachments you still have with your former spouse and how this might impact your new marriage.

Much of your personal readiness for remarriage depends on the state of your relationship with your former spouse, whether he or she is deceased or you are divorced. What lessons from your first marriage will you bring into your second marriage? Is there unresolved pain in relation to your first spouse that you need to work through? Before entering into a new marriage, carefully examine the baggage you are bringing with you.[7]

46. What was your last marriage like?

What are three reasons you're confident the relationship is over (whether by death or divorce) so you can move forward?

•

•

•

It's important that people grieve over broken relationships and are able to say goodbye. They need to be 100 percent sure the relationship is over. If they are still thinking about their former partners, this is not a good sign. If they say, "I just know it's over," don't accept that as a substitute for providing specific reasons.

Did you and/or your partner complete a "Divorce Care" program? If not, you may want to look into it.

Ghosts are the internal feelings or reactions people have to external objects, occurrences, or memories. Furniture, family pictures, flashbacks, handiwork habits, cooking, decorating, comparisons, using the wrong name—any of these things can trigger such a response. A courting couple needs to be aware that some of these feelings will inevitably appear.

Ghosts of the past are often evoked unthinkingly by the mates themselves. An embarrassing moment for any couple is calling the new partner by the previous partner's name. When conversations turn to former mates, it can upset one or both of you.

Steps omitted or not completed in the grieving process can also come back to haunt a person's new relationship. When ghosts appear, be empathetic and kind to each other.

47. What ghosts might appear in your new marriage? How will you handle them?

48. What are your partner's preferences concerning family pictures from the previous relationship, living in the same house as before, and using the same furniture?

What are your preferences when it comes to these issues?

Whether past family photographs project the active presence of the people into the lives of the new couple depends much on where they are located because this indicates their degree of importance. A positive solution two couples found was to assemble a picture gallery of the two families—leaving out no one. One has it in a finished basement recreation room, the other one located the photographs in the main floor hallway so the children could maintain a sense of biological continuity and relationship.

49. What, if any, losses in your life have you not fully grieved over?

We've all experienced loss. If they haven't been grieved for when they occurred, they will come back and often intensify the emotions during the next loss. Unresolved losses can interfere with relationships, especially if they were the result of rejection.

Do both of you have a healthy pattern of grieving? You'll need this for the future. Be sure to discuss this together. For additional help, read my book *Recovering from the Losses of Life*.

50. These are the activities I enjoy doing (list them):

Go through this activity list with your partner and put a check mark by the ones he or she wouldn't enjoy doing with you.

Now repeat the exercise with your partner's activities list.

Many couples discover that their partners never really enjoyed some of the activities they participated in with them during their dating time. They got involved just to be together. This ends up being "courtship deception" because it sends the message that "I like doing this now so I will continue to participate after we're married." Clear the air now. Each of you will probably have your own separate hobbies as well as activities you do together. If there are no activities you currently enjoy doing together, how will you unwind or spend recreational time together once you're married?

Another great question is how much emphasis or priority both of you place on your activities. Will the hobbies or interests interfere with your relationship? Will you or your partner resent time spent on the activities or with the people who participate in them? Even good things can become detrimental when and if they take on too much importance. Balance is the key.

51. What habits does your partner have, good or bad?

52. Who are your partner's heroes? Why do you think your partner admires them or trusts them?

53. What was the lowest point or most difficult time in your life?

How did you handle it?

It takes trust to share openly in this area. Treat what your partner says as a gift and handle the information and emotions carefully. Sometimes sharing about this may answer other questions you have. We all carry scars from the past, but if there's still an open wound, it may be best to wait for healing to happen before you deepen your relationship.

54. When and under what circumstances have you been depressed? How did this impact your life?

Have you experienced any other emotional issues? Explain.

Have any of your family members experienced depression or other emotional issues? Explain.

Depression is a normal response to many of life's events. Being aware of your family's depression history may give you insights and even answers regarding your own depression. Letting your partner know how you want him or her to respond when you're depressed is also important. And it's just as important for you to be aware of your partner's experiences in this area. For more information on depression be sure to read *Breaking Through Depression* by Donald Hall.

55. Describe how you handle stress and frustration.

What creates the most stresses and frustrations in your life?

When you and your partner share, be sure to notice whether your partner's response to stress and frustration is healthy and nonthreatening. Would you be concerned if your family or friends saw your partner's reaction and behavior? Is this a response you can live with for the rest of your life? If you have children, do you want them to observe this behavior and follow that pattern? Does your partner have a positive handle on dealing with these issues or is more work needed?

56. How will you handle holidays, birthdays, special occasions, and such when it comes to your two families, as well as your former families?

What does gift giving mean and generally require in your family?

Now is the time to discuss traditions and expectations. What does your partner want to continue and discontinue? How flexible will your families be to changes you may want to make? What if gifts are very important to you, but the other family doesn't give any? Or what if they give lavish gifts and you have a set monetary limit? Sometimes these issues need to be discussed with the children involved as well.

57. What are three ways in which you see us as different?

What are three ways in which you see us as similar?

Which of these six items are you comfortable with?

Couples are drawn together by differences as well as similarities. Sometimes we respond because people fill our empty places. Sometimes we're comfortable with similarities. You may look at one another's differences now and say, "Oh, you're so *unique!*" But after a couple of years of marriage you may say, "I knew you were different—but not this much!" You may come to see the differences as wrong and set out on a crusade to make the other person into a closer rendition of yourself.

Do you celebrate your differences now? If you don't, you won't later. Consider this Scripture for your relationship: "Be humble and gentle. Be patient with each other, making allowance for each other's faults because of your love. Try always to be led along together by the Holy Spirit and so be at peace with one another" (Ephesians 4:2-3 TLB).

58. If I tell you I don't want to do something or that I don't feel comfortable doing something you want to do, how will you handle that?

   Differences will arise. Each person brings personal preferences to a relationship that may be foreign to the other. Some may be all right, some may be questionable, and others may not fit into the partner's Christian framework. How will each of you handle a "no" from the other? Now is the time to find out.

59. Everyone brings some baggage into relationships. What baggage are you bringing? Would it fit into an attaché case, a carry-on bag, a small suitcase, or a trunk? Explain.

We would all like to have our baggage fit in the attaché case, but nowadays they are expandable! Is the person you're interested in characterized by the term "walking wounded"? Are you? This is a person who is carrying a load of baggage. Baggage will interfere with the marriage.[8] Among the baggage could be rejection, abuse, promiscuity, homosexuality, substance abuse, financial problems, former in-laws, former spouse, work or relationship instability, erratic faith practices, and so on. What's important is knowing there *is* baggage, identifying its potential effects, and taking corrective steps to move forward in life.

60. How do you feel about discussing burial plans before marriage?

For older couples with grown children, this may not sound so far-fetched. Sometimes one or both parties have made investments in family plots long before the new marriage. What will be done with the already purchased sites? How will you and your partner handle previous plans made with others? Who will be buried beside whom?

Most of the older couples I've known choose to be buried with their previous mates. This reflected economic factors, consideration for their children, and other personal motives.

Discussing final plans isn't macabre or somber. When you handle serious questions sensibly, both of you can move into your new marriage with greater security and comfort.

61. What issues have you and your current partner already argued about?

What do you think will be three issues you will argue about when you marry your current partner?

What creates these arguments, and what would be healthy ways to resolve them?

62. How comfortable are you with confrontation or conflict? How do you usually resolve them?

> Conflict is an opportunity to get better acquainted, a chance to learn something about the background, history, experiences or beliefs of the person you've married. Rather than burying or avoiding conflict, bringing it to the light allows a couple to learn about each other, serve and encourage each other, and grow closer and deeper in their relationship.[9]

One of you may be accustomed to confrontation, and for the other it may be new. It may be second nature and a positive experience in your relationship or a sign that it is in trouble. Perhaps you've wanted to discuss this but have been afraid to move in that direction. Talk about it today.

63. Where does anger enter into your relationship?

How do you express anger?

How does your partner express anger?

Anger expressed in a healthy, non-attacking way can build a relationship. Repressed or constantly held-in anger will eventually damage the person and the relationship.

64. When you marry, do you want more children? If so, how many? Are you open to adoption? What training have you had to be a parent, stepparent, or stepgrandparent?

Having children will change the relationship more than you realize. Your couple time together will be reduced by about 80 percent. Why do each of you want children? Discuss all aspects of childrearing, including number, care, finances, adoption, and so forth. Work toward a resolution now. Please be open to taking classes and reading books together about stepparenting if that will be part of your life together.

65. How do your children feel about the possibility of you remarrying?

Have both of you offered reassurance of your love and continuing concern to your own children and to the children of your future spouse? How will you help your children understand that no one can replace their other parent, but that your new partner will add strength and blessing to their lives if they allow it to happen?

66. As you think about getting remarried, are you secretly (or openly) hoping to gain a new disciplinarian around the house? Do you hope that bringing a new "mom" or "dad" into the home will teach your children how to behave themselves? If you and your partner both have children at home, are you content to let each other keep on disciplining your respective children in your own ways?

What do you think of the recommendation by many remarried families—as well as marriage and family therapists—of "letting the birth parent be the boss parent"? Think about this: Are you willing to wait to be liked until later? Are you willing to be "tough" and "firm" in the early days of your remarriage, following the birth parent's rules and practices, even if the children seem angry with you?[10] What will you do if one of you is stricter than the other, and the children complain about the disparity?

67. What will your relationships be like with your parents, siblings, friends, and former family members after you marry? Will they be the same or different? If different, in what ways?

Before taking the big step, spend time with your partner's family in all types of settings. Are the interactions you see loving and positive or strained and obligatory? How do these compare with your experiences? Their family members will be a part of your life too. Time spent with each family will be diminished, but what gatherings will be part of your new life together?

68. Because the issues that will come if both of you (or one of you) have kids from previous marriages are so important, let's review how you will handle them.

What will you call the former partners when they call or visit?

What rules will you have for phone contact and personal visits by former partners?

Should former partners be allowed in your home? Should you visit your former partners in their homes?

How will you handle disagreements over the care of the children and activities in which former partners are involved?

What will you do if one of the children or stepchildren wants to change residence?

How do you feel about the types of gifts former partners bring to the children or ex-spouses?

What visiting privileges will you give to the relatives of your former partner who consider your children or stepchildren part of their families?

How will you talk to your children or stepchildren about your former partner's motives and actions that you believe to be wrong?

What will you ask your children to say when your former partner asks about their new family relationships?

What will you say about your new family when people ask about the new relationship?

What is your plan for handling holidays, birthdays, and special occasions? How will you handle your desires and your former partner's desires if they conflict?

What will you share with your children about their new relatives they have inherited?

What additional issues do you feel need to be thought through prior to your marriage?

Describe how you have listened to and responded to your children's concerns about your future marriage.

69. If you marry, what do you think will be the hardest adjustment for your partner to make to live with you in peaceful harmony?

Don't expect an immediate answer to this question. Suggest that your partner reflect on it for a while. What they suggest could be a revelation to you or it could be something you expected. What is it that neither of you could handle?

70. How much do you value "personal time"—time to yourself to reflect, study, or recreate?

Which of you tends to be more of a loner?

How will you handle the differences between you?

If your partner is an introvert—one who is drained by people and needs quiet, private time to recharge—and you're an extrovert, you'll need to work on understanding and accepting these differences, as well as not invading each other's private times. Or you could be the introvert, and your partner needs to be with people far more than you. Understanding how each other operates is the key. See my book *Communication: Key to Your Marriage* for more insights on this.

71. What are your financial responsibilities and goals?

How capable are you in budgeting? Balancing the checkbook? Sticking to a budget when shopping? How stressful are these things to you?

What debts do you have at this time? Have you ever filed for bankruptcy or defaulted on a loan?

Finances are at the heart of so many conflicts in relationships. You need to know what the other one earns, as well as his or her earning potential. And your partner needs to know that about you. Has each of you used a budget? If not, begin working on one now if you proceed in your relationship.

Is shopping a planned activity with financial resources in mind or is it often a credit-card binge? Is shopping a delight or a chore?

If a bankruptcy or loan default has occurred, it could affect future credit. What are your respective credit scores? If this area will be problematic, talk to a financial consultant about solutions.

How will you approach any obligations to a former spouse or children?

72. What has been the greatest amount of debt you've experienced? This could have been a one-time debt or it could be an ongoing accumulation that keeps building.

Are you expected to help with your partner's debt? How do you feel about that? Do you have concerns about your partner pulling you into unwanted debt?

Money management in a remarriage can become a nightmare. If there are children from a previous marriage, financial support becomes a burden to the remarriage. Consider this fact: Approximately 1 in 10 children live with their biological father and a stepmother. Because of this, the typical remarrying father will enter the remarriage with up to 20 years of financial obligation. Each month he will send a check to another woman. If his new wife has her own children, he will also be helping to support her children.

P.S. *Remember this about money:* God is the one who owns everything. You are a steward of His resources. He wants you to use them wisely and in such a way that it's a positive reflection on Him.

73. How do you know you're in love with your partner?

Here are some healthy indications of love:

▶ *Sharing test:* Are you able to share together?

▶ *Strength test:* Does your love give you new strength and fill you with creative energy? Or does it take away your strength and energy?

▶ *Respect test:* Do you respect each other?

▶ *Habit test:* Do you only *love* each other—or do you *like* each other and accept each other, including habits and shortcomings?

▶ *Time test:* Have you known each other long enough to know each other well?

▶ *Separation test:* Do you feel an unusual joy while in the company of each other? Is there pain during separations?

▶ *Giving test:* Are you in love to give? Are you capable of giving yourself?

▶ *Growth test:* Is your love dynamic in its growth? Is it progressively maturing?

▶ *Sex test:* Is there mutual enjoyment of each other without the constant need of physical expression?

74. What do you think Ephesians 5:22 and 25 means? "Wives, submit yourselves to your own husbands" and "Husbands, love your wives, just as Christ loved the church and gave himself up for her"?

An understanding of this biblical teaching is paramount. Too often neither party has studied these passages in depth. Take the time to discuss them with knowledgeable individuals. These roles talk about each person's responsibility, not each person's value. Remember, both of you have equal value before God.

75. Who are you? How would you describe who you are to someone?

For many this is difficult. They may describe personal characteristics and work ability from a spiritual dimension. We all need to know who we are and where we are going in life. Do you?

76. What life experiences do you want your partner to have had?

What life experiences would you not want your partner to have had?

Do those seem like strange questions? They aren't, really. You may think your partner is too sheltered or has been around too much. You might discover you're really different. How will this affect a lifelong relationship? Can you learn from one another? Do you believe your partner is damaged by these experiences or is naïve? Your response to their replies is critical. Your dreams and expectations may need to be adjusted.

77. Who are the remarried couples you know who have growing, healthy marriages?

If neither of you can think of any, please begin looking. If all you know are negative and dysfunctional couples, that could impact your relationship. It's important to see how Jesus Christ can make a difference in marriages. Happy remarried couples *do* exist!

78. On a scale from 0 to 10, to what extent do you experience guilt or anguish over your previous marriage?

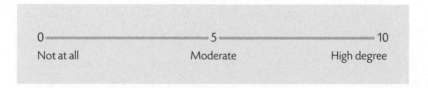

0 ——————————————— 5 ——————————————— 10
Not at all   Moderate   High degree

Is your guilt or anguish realistic? What does it stem from?

How might this guilt affect building a marriage with your new partner?

If your partner has issues related to a previous relationship, has he or she discussed the relationship with someone who can help?

To have a fulfilling relationship for the future, the ghosts of past relationships need to be put to rest. A new relationship is not a solution for guilt; experiencing God's forgiveness is.

79. What are your hobbies and interests, aside from work? How much time and energy go into these? Will this change or stay the same when you marry? If you spend a lot of time on the computer, cell phone, or Facebook, how will you adjust this to work in a marriage?

Does your partner have any hobbies or is he or she a workaholic? What if your partner doesn't have hobbies, but you do? How will he or she handle your time spent on your hobbies? If your partner is very involved in some activities, will that continue at the same level?

You can't bring the single lifestyle into a marriage relationship. Is there something the two of you are open to exploring together? If your partner is very involved in some activities, will they expect to continue this involvement at the same level if they marry?

80. If you were to marry, what would you receive from marriage that you wouldn't have if you were to remain single?

What are the unique issues to face if one of you has been married three times and the other once?

Don't accept just a few basic, brief responses to these questions. Encourage your partner to think about these for a while. There are many benefits to remarriage, and it helps to identify them now. It may also reduce some of the fears that keep people from making commitments.

81. What has been your source of information about remarriage? Parents, friends, classes, books? Which has had the most significant impact? Why?

What will you do to learn more about marriage after you're married?

How has your former marriage impacted your beliefs about marriage?

We all learn about marriage through the years. Is your knowledge accurate? Positive? Will it help or hinder the marital growth process? If your partner has never read a book on marriage, there are plenty of resources to choose from. So it's time to get to work and expand your understanding of marriage. See the recommended reading list at the end of this book.

82. What are the areas of your life you *must* control and those areas in your life you would *like* to control?

If your partner says, "I'm not in control of anything in life," watch out. If your partner says, "I must be in control of everything in my life," watch out—that might include you. We all like to be in control in some areas, but few have thought this through. We're not really in control as much as we think we are. What's best is to learn to let God control our lives. And by the way, are you aware that the number one reason for love dying after marriage is a controlling spouse? It's something to think about.

83. What television programs and movies have made an impact on your life? Explain. How much time do you spend watching TV? How about your partner?

Since movies and TV influence society and culture, they can also shape our personal beliefs, desires, and values. Listen to your partner's program selection. It speaks volumes about who and what has impacted him or her. Are your tastes similar or dissimilar? Could you spend the rest of your life watching and listening to the same programs? If you were to marry, who would be in charge of the remote? Could you live without a TV? All of these are significant questions to discuss before marriage.

84. During a conflict, a person either yields, withdraws, compromises, wins, or resolves. Which of these tends to be your style?

Which tends to be your partner's style?

"What causes fights and quarrels among you? Don't they come from your desires that battle within you? You desire but do not have, so you kill. You covet but you cannot get what you want, so you quarrel and fight. You do not have because you do not ask God. When you ask, you do not receive, because you ask with wrong motives, that you may spend what you get on your pleasures" (James 4:1-3). There will be numerous conflicts throughout the life of a marriage. This isn't bad; it's normal. How you respond and deal with them is the real issue. How have they been resolved so far? They can be opportunities for growth in a relationship, but not if you always yield, withdraw, attempt to win, or even compromise. Work toward resolving the conflict so you both have your needs met and are satisfied with the resolution.

85. What was the best experience you've ever had at church?

What was the worst?

How involved do you want to be in a local church? Whose church will you attend if you come from different churches? Often we let past experiences dictate our future. This can be positive or negative. If you're together in your level of involvement in church, it can draw you closer together.

86. Describe how you came to know the Lord. When was it? Who was involved? Where did it take place? How has your life changed?

For some, their conversion was dramatic, and for others it was very casual. For spiritual compatibility to develop, you need to know how each of you became a believer and where you are in this lifelong journey. It may take some time for your partner to reflect on this question.

87. What do you believe are five elements that make marriages work? Explain.

Perhaps your beliefs are similar...or they could be radically different. Once you identify them, you can discuss how you would make sure these elements exist and continue to be enhanced. On the other hand, if there is no awareness of them, perhaps you need to investigate. One fundamental element should be *dedication,* which, according to author and relationship expert Dr. Scott Stanley, is motivation based on a thoughtful decision to follow a certain path and give it your best. Have you experienced this or seen it occur in your partner?

88. In light of the number of divorces today, why would your new marriage last and not end up in divorce court?

Love is not enough, and being Christians doesn't guarantee success. You have to make your relationship a priority at all times. Marriage is a covenant—an unconditional commitment to an imperfect person, which means sticking to marriage and one another rather than ending up stuck. If your partner (or you) doesn't have a game plan at this time, you need to get one.

89. What have been your experiences with alcohol and/or drugs in the past? How about at the present time?

If there has been drug or alcohol use, what kind, to what extent, how recent was the usage, how did it stop—was there a treatment program—and what is your partner's intent for the future? You should also see if drug or alcohol use runs in the family.

90. Of all the emotions we experience in life, what are the easiest ones for you to express?

What are the most difficult?

Everyone is an emotional being. Some experience or express emotions more intensely than others. Some children are raised without an emotional or feeling vocabulary, so it is difficult for them as adults to express what they are experiencing inside. Talk about each of the following: fear, worry, anxiety, depression, sadness, anger, rage, frustration, guilt, shame, delight, sorrow, joy. (This will keep you busy for a while).

91. What are the passions in life you would love doing, and which of those would be meaningful to you if I were to do them with you?

Togetherness in a relationship means being able to play, work, and serve together. Are each of you willing to at least try the other's passion? If nothing clicks, both of you could try something new in order to discover an interest you can do together. If there is nothing, and you go ahead and marry, you could end up as a pair of married singles.

92. What foods do you enjoy?

What are your feelings about eating healthy?

Can food and diet really be a problem? Definitely, especially if one partner is weight-conscious or into the healthiest foods and the other is a fast-food junkie on his or her way to breaking the high-cholesterol record.

When you marry, how often will you eat in or go out? Who will have the final say on meals? And by the way, can either of you cook?

93. Politically, where do you find yourself—liberal, middle of the road, conservative, ultraconservative? Using the same scale, where do you find yourself spiritually?

Perhaps neither of you has ever labeled yourself politically before, but you need to think about it. Where does each of you stand on abortion and same-sex marriages? These issues are political and spiritual. Do you both need to agree in this area or can you allow differences? As you discuss these issues, make sure both of you give ample support for your beliefs. Also, who has influenced these beliefs?

94. Do you feel you need to compromise or sacrifice anything to be a part of this relationship?

Relationships are based on give and take. They can't consist of all taking and no giving or all giving and no taking. Balance is key. Make sure you learn what strikes balance in the give-and-take area for the both of you. Be wary if your partner feels his or her life is one giant compromise.

95. What are the five biggest fears in your life?

This can be a very revealing question. Couples can be married for years and never be aware their partner has any fears. How do these fears affect your relationship? How could you assist one another in overcoming fears?

96. Do you like animals? What animal would you love to have as a pet that you don't or can't have at this time? How will you work it out if your partner wants an animal and you don't?

It's not just the animals that can be the issue. It's also where they live and who takes care of them. What if one of you has allergies or fears about certain animals? When you marry, what animals will be brought into the marriage?

97. Who are the people in your life you've needed to forgive, and how did you accomplish this?

Who do you still need to forgive?

Forgiveness is essential in any relationship. Have you seen forgiveness occur in your relationship or is your partner a grudge collector? Resentment will poison a relationship—even resentment toward those other than you. Forgiveness is a process and may take time. Both of you will need an abundance of this skill if you marry. You'll learn it by experiencing God's forgiveness.

98. Take note of the fruit of the Spirit found in Galatians 5:22-23: "love, joy, peace, forbearance, kindness, goodness, faithfulness, gentleness and self-control." On a scale from 0 to 10, where do you see yourself on each of these traits at this point in your life?

- Love:

- Joy:

- Peace:

- Forbearance:

- Kindness:

- Goodness:

- Faithfulness:

- Gentleness:

- Self-control:

A relationship built on the teachings in God's Word has the best foundation for a fulfilling and lasting marriage. Do you look to the Scriptures as the basis for the way to respond to one another? If not, it's not too late to begin.

99. Do you believe you and your partner should be honest about everything in your relationship or should some things be kept private?

If asked if you were honest and trustworthy, how would your past partner(s) answer?

Sometimes people let things slide during courtship in order to not rock the boat. Partners sometimes even think they'll be able to sway their partners after the marriage ceremony. It doesn't work. You need a partner who is truthful and doesn't bend the truth in any way. You need a partner who is honest with him- or herself and doesn't practice self-deception. You need a person who is honest with you.

100. After answering and discussing all these questions, are there some areas that need further discussion? What would you like to discuss in more detail?

Take the time to go over these problem areas, discuss them thoroughly, pray together and separately about them, and then discuss them again.

101. Are you confident there is a healthy future for both of you? What do
you envision in the future for this relationship?

Make sure you take time to celebrate all you do have in common. You
should now have a good foundation for building a life together. If you
discover that you're not as compatible as you first thought, or if too many
red flags were raised during your discussions, it's best to know that now
and back out of the relationship rather than end up in an unhealthy marriage to a stranger. If you've decided you're even more compatible than you
thought, prayerfully move forward.

Recommended Reading

Cloud, Henry, and John Townsend. *Boundaries in Dating.* Grand Rapids, MI: Zondervan, 2000.

Kniskern, Joseph Warren. *Making a New Vow: A Christian's Guide to Remarriage.* Nashville: B & H Publishing Group, 2003.

Larson, Jeffrey. *Should We Stay Together?* Hoboken, NJ: John Wiley & Sons, 2000.

Parrott, Les and Leslie. *Saving Your Marriage Before It Starts.* Grand Rapids, MI: Zondervan, 2006.

Phillips, Bob. *How Can I Be Sure?* Eugene, OR: Harvest House, 1999.

Tauber, Edward M., and Jim Smoke. *Finding the Right One After Divorce.* Eugene, OR: Harvest House, 2007.

Warren, Rick. *The Purpose-Driven Life.* Grand Rapids, MI: Zondervan, 2002.

Wright, H. Norman. *Before You Say "I Do" Devotional.* Eugene, OR: Harvest House, 2003.

_____. *Communication: Key to Your Marriage.* Ventura, CA: Regal Books, 2000.

_____. *Starting Out Together.* Ventura, CA: Regal Books, 1996.

Notes

Chapter 1: Establishing a Solid Foundation

1. Barbara De Angelis, PhD, *Are You the One for Me?* (New York: Delacorte Press, 1992), 91-100.

2. H. Norman Wright, *Relationships that Work (and Those that Don't)* (Ventura, CA: Regal Books, 1998), 116-18.

3. Rachel Safiew with Wendy Roberts, *There Goes the Bride* (San Francisco: John Wiley & Sons, Inc., 2003), 5-10, 119.

4. Jeffrey H. Larson, *Should We Stay Together* (Indianapolis: Jossey-Bass, 2000), 165-66, adapted.

Chapter 2: Previous Relationships

1. Edward M. Tauber and Jim Smoke, *Finding the Right One After Divorce* (Eugene, OR: Harvest House Publishers, 2007), 28-30, adapted.

2. Les and Leslie Parrott, *Saving Your Second Marriage Before It Starts* (Grand Rapids, MI: Zondervan, 2001), 30-31.

Chapter 3: 101 Questions to Help You Develop Your Relationship

1. Tauber and Smoke, *Finding the Right One*, 196.

2. Parrott and Parrott, Saving *Your Second Marriage*, 20-21, adapted.

3. Ibid., 24.

4. Dr. Paul Tournier, *The Healing of Persons* (New York: Harper Collins, 1965), 88.

5. Dr. Dwight Small, *After You've Said I Do* (Westwood, NJ: Fleming H. Revell, 1968), 75.

6. Parrot and Parrott, *Saving Your Second Marriage,* 160.

7. Ibid., 25.

8. Tauber and Smoke, *Finding the Right One,* 28-30, adapted.

9. David and Lisa Frisbie, *Happily Remarried* (Eugene, OR: Harvest House Publishers, 2005), 78.

10. Ibid., 221-22.